101 Powerful Bible Verses

Glen R. Landin

Copyright © 2014 Glen R. Landin.

No part of this publication may be reproduced or transmitted in any form or by any means, electronic or mechanical, including photocopying, recording, or by any information storage or retrieval system without written permission from the publisher.

Scriptures NIV are from The Holy Bible, New International Version®. © 1973, 1978, 1984 by International Bible Society. All rights reserved.

CREATIVEARTISTIC PUBLISHING
WWW.CREATIVEARTISTICPUBLISHING.COM
ORANGE, CALIFORNIA

ISBN 978-0615912790

PRINTED EDITION: JANUARY 2014

PRINTED IN THE UNITED STATES OF AMERICA

WWW.GLENLANDIN.COM

GLEN R. LANDIN

The 101 Powerful Bible Verses comprises the most important verses from each book of The Holy Bible. This book also includes a bold silhouette cross, and the first and last verses. Perfect for Bible studies, memorization, and personal spiritual growth and reflection.

101 POWERFUL BIBLE VERSES

In the beginning God created the heavens and the earth.

Genesis 1:1 (NIV)

GLEN R. LANDIN

So God created human beings in his own image, in the image of God he created them; male and female he created them.

Genesis 1:27 (NIV)

By the seventh day God had finished the work he had been doing; so on the seventh day he rested from all his work.

Genesis 2:2 (NIV)

GLEN R. LANDIN

"God said to Moses, "I AM WHO I AM.
This is what you are to say to the
Israelites: "I AM has sent me to you"

Exodus 3:14 (NIV)

101 POWERFUL BIBLE VERSES

"Remember the Sabbath day by keeping it holy."

Exodus 20:8 (NIV)

GLEN R. LANDIN

You are to lay your hand on the head of the burnt offering, and it will be accepted on your behalf to make atonement for you.

Leviticus 1:4 (NIV)

"A tithe of everything from the land, whether grain from the soil or fruit from the trees, belongs to the LORD; it is holy to the LORD."

Leviticus 27:30 (NIV)

GLEN R. LANDIN

"Take a census of the whole Israelite community by their clans and families, listing every man by name, one by one."

Numbers 1:2 (NIV)

*"The LORD bless you and keep you;"
The LORD make his face shine on you
and be gracious to you; The LORD turn
his face toward you and give you peace."*

Numbers 6:24-26 (NIV)

GLEN R. LANDIN

*Love the LORD your God with all
your heart and with all your soul
and with all your strength.*

Deuteronomy 6:5 (NIV)

"Have I not commanded you? Be strong and courageous. Do not be afraid; do not be discouraged, for the LORD your God will be with you wherever you go."

Joshua 1:9 (NIV)

GLEN R. LANDIN

"He sent them a prophet, who said, "This is what the LORD, the God of Israel, says: I brought you up out of Egypt, out of the land of slavery."

Judges 6:8 (NIV)

But Ruth replied, "Don't urge me to leave you or to turn back from you. Where you go I will go, and where you stay I will stay. Your people will be my people and your God my God."

Ruth 1:16 (NIV)

GLEN R. LANDIN

"*Do not keep talking so proudly or
let your mouth speak such arrogance,
for the LORD is a God who knows,
and by him deeds are weighed.*"

1 Samuel 2:3 (NIV)

When your days are over and you rest with your ancestors, I will raise up your offspring to succeed you, who will come from your own body, and I will establish his kingdom.

2 Samuel 7:12 (NIV)

GLEN R. LANDIN

When the priests withdrew from the Holy Place, the cloud filled the temple of the LORD.

1 Kings 8:10 (NIV)

As they were walking along and talking together, suddenly a chariot of fire and horses of fire appeared and separated the two of them, and Elijah went up to heaven in a whirlwind.

2 Kings 2:11 (NIV)

GLEN R. LANDIN

David told the leaders of the Levites to appoint their fellow Levites as musicians to make a joyful sound with musical instruments: lyres, harps, and cymbals.

1 Chronicles 15:16 (NIV)

LORD. For the sake of your servant and according to your will, you have done this great thing and made known all these great promises.

1 Chronicles 17:19 (NIV)

GLEN R. LANDIN

Solomon went up to the bronze alter before the LORD in the tent of meeting and offered a thousand burnt offerings on it.

2 Chronicles 1:6 (NIV)

On the eighth day they held an assembly, for they had celebrated the dedication of the alter for seven days and the festival for seven days more.

2 Chronicles 7:9 (NIV)

GLEN R. LANDIN

For Ezra had devoted himself to the study and observance of the Law of the LORD, and to teaching its decrees and laws in Israel.

Ezra 7:10 (NIV)

When I heard these things, I sat down and wept. For some days I mourned and fasted and prayed before the God of heaven.

Nehemiah 1:4 (NIV)

GLEN R. LANDIN

For a full 180 days he displayed the vast wealth of his kingdom and the splendor and glory of his majesty.

Esther 1:4 (NIV)

One day the angels came to present themselves before the LORD, and Satan also came with them.

Job 1:6 (NIV)

GLEN R. LANDIN

I know that my redeemer lives, and that in the end he will stand on the earth.

Job 19:25 (NIV)

I sought the LORD, and he answered me; he delivered me from all my fears.

Psalms 34:4 (NIV)

GLEN R. LANDIN

Taste and see that the LORD is good; blessed is the one who takes refuge in him.

Psalms 34:8 (NIV)

Take delight in the LORD and he will give you the desires of your heart.

Psalms 37:4 (NIV)

GLEN R. LANDIN

*"Be still, and know that I am God;
I will be exalted among the nations,
I will be exalted in the earth."*

Psalms 46:10 (NIV)

*The LORD has done it this very day;
let us rejoice today and be glad.*

Psalms 118:24 (NIV)

GLEN R. LANDIN

The fear of the LORD is the beginning of knowledge, but fools despise wisdom and instruction.

Proverbs 1:7 (NIV)

Trust in the LORD with all your heart and lean not on your own understanding.

Proverbs 3:5 (NIV)

GLEN R. LANDIN

*Commit to the LORD whatever you do,
and he will establish your plans.*

Proverbs 16:3 (NIV)

There is no wisdom, no insight, no plan that can succeed against the LORD.

Proverbs 21:30 (NIV)

GLEN R. LANDIN

"Every word of God is flawless, he is a shield to those who take refuge in him."

Proverbs 30:5 (NIV)

Now all has been heard; here is the conclusion of the matter: Fear God and keep his commandments, for this is the duty of every human being.

Ecclesiastes 12:13 (NIV)

GLEN R. LANDIN

Let him kiss me with the kisses of his mouth – for your love is more delightful than wine.

Song of Solomon 1:2 (NIV)

*And they were calling to one another:
"Holy, holy, holy is the LORD Almighty;
the whole earth is full of his glory."*

Isaiah 6:3 (NIV)

GLEN R. LANDIN

Therefore the LORD himself will give you a sign: The virgin will conceive and give birth to a son, and will call him Immanuel.

Isaiah 7:14 (NIV)

For to us a child is born, to us a son is given, and the government will be on his shoulders. And he will be called Wonderful Counselor, Mighty God, Everlasting Father, Prince of Peace.

Isaiah 9:6 (NIV)

GLEN R. LANDIN

But those who hope in the LORD will renew their strength. They will soar on wings like eagles; they will run and not grow weary, they will walk and not be faint.

Isaiah 40:31 (NIV)

*"For I know the plans I have for you,"
declares the LORD, "plans to prosper
you and not to harm you, plans to
give you hope and a future."*

Jeremiah 29:11 (NIV)

GLEN R. LANDIN

*Because of the LORD's great love
we are not consumed, for his
compassions never fail.*

Lamentations 3:22 (NIV)

I will give you a new heart and put a new spirit in you; I will remove from you your heart of stone and give you a heart of flesh.

Ezekiel 36:26 (NIV)

GLEN R. LANDIN

Multitudes who sleep in the dust of the earth will awake; some to everlasting life, others to shame and everlasting contempt.

Daniel 12:2 (NIV)

For I desire mercy, not sacrifice, and acknowledgement of God rather than burnt offerings.

Hosea 6:6 (NIV)

GLEN R. LANDIN

"Even now," declares the LORD, "return to me with all your heart, with fasting and weeping and mourning."

Joel 2:12 (NIV)

Surely the Sovereign LORD does nothing without revealing his plan to his servants the prophets.

Amos 3:7 (NIV)

GLEN R. LANDIN

"The day of the LORD is near for all nations. As you have done, it will be done to you; your deeds will return upon your own head."

Obadiah 1:15 (NIV)

Then the LORD sent a great wind on the sea, and such a violent storm arose that the ship threatened to break up.

Jonah 1:4 (NIV)

GLEN R. LANDIN

Hear, you peoples, all of you, listen, earth and all who live in it, that the Sovereign LORD may witness against you, the LORD from his holy temple.

Micah 1:2 (NIV)

The LORD is good, a refuge in times of trouble. He cares for those who trust in him.

Nahum 1:7 (NIV)

GLEN R. LANDIN

*His splendor was like the sunrise;
rays flashed from his hand, where
his power was hidden.*

Habakkuk 3:4 (NIV)

"The LORD your God is with you, the Mighty Warrior who saves. He will take great delight in you; in his love he will no longer rebuke you, but will rejoice over you with singing."

Zephaniah 3:17 (NIV)

GLEN R. LANDIN

"This is what I covenanted with you when you came out of Egypt. And my Spirit remains among you. Do not fear."

Haggai 2:5 (NIV)

The LORD will be king over the whole earth. On that day there will be one LORD, and his name the only name.

Zechariah 14:9 (NIV)

GLEN R. LANDIN

You will see it with your own eyes and say, "Great is the LORD – even beyond the borders of Israel!"

Malachi 1:5 (NIV)

On coming to the house, they saw the child with his mother Mary and they bowed down and worshiped him. Then they opened their treasures and presented him with gifts of gold, frankincense, and myrrh.

Matthew 21:22 (NIV)

GLEN R. LANDIN

Therefore go and make disciples of all nations, baptizing then in the name of the Father and of the Son and of the Holy Spirit.

Matthew 28:19 (NIV)

*Love the LORD your God
with all your heart and with
all your soul and with all your
mind and with all your strength.*

Mark 12:29 (NIV)

GLEN R. LANDIN

Whoever believes and is baptized will be saved, but whoever does not believe will be condemned.

Mark 16:16 (NIV)

And there were shepherd's living out in the fields nearby, keeping watch over their flocks at night. An angel of the LORD appeared to them, and the glory of the LORD shone around them, and they were terrified. But the angel said to them, "Do not be afraid. I bring you good news that will cause great joy for all the people."
Luke 2:8-10 (NIV)

GLEN R. LANDIN

"Give, and it will be given to you. A good measure, pressed down, shaken together and running over, will be poured into your lap. For with the measure you use, it will be measured to you."

Luke 6:38 (NIV)

For God so loved the world that he gave his one and only Son, that whoever believes in him shall not perish but have eternal life.

John 3:16 (NIV)

GLEN R. LANDIN

Jesus answered, "I am the way and the truth and the life. No one comes to the Father except through me."

John 14:6 (NIV)

"But you will receive power when the Holy Spirit comes on you; and you will be my witness in Jerusalem, and in all Judea and Samaria, and to the ends of the earth."

Acts 1:8 (NIV)

GLEN R. LANDIN

They replied, "Believe in the Lord Jesus, and you will be saved — you and your household."

Acts 16:31 (NIV)

For all have sinned and fall short of the glory of God.

Romans 3:23 (NIV)

GLEN R. LANDIN

For the wages of sin is death, but the gift of God is eternal life in Christ Jesus our Lord.

Romans 6:23 (NIV)

*Love is patient, love is kind.
It does not envy, it does not
boast, it is not proud.*

1 Corinthians 13:4 (NIV)

GLEN R. LANDIN

And now these three remain: faith, hope and love. But the greatest of these is love.

1 Corinthians 13:13 (NIV)

Therefore, if anyone is in Christ, the new creation has come: The old has gone, the new is here!

2 Corinthians 5:17 (NIV)

GLEN R. LANDIN

*May the grace of the Lord Jesus Christ,
and the love of God, and the fellowship
of the Holy Spirit be with you all.*

2 Corinthians 13:14 (NIV)

101 POWERFUL BIBLE VERSES

But the fruit of the Spirit is love, joy, peace, patience, kindness, goodness, faithfulness.

Galatians 5:22 (NIV)

GLEN R. LANDIN

Do not be deceived: God cannot be mocked. People reap what they sow.

Galatians 6:7 (NIV)

For it is by grace you have been saved, through faith — and this is not from yourselves, it is the gift of God.

Ephesians 2:8 (NIV)

GLEN R. LANDIN

For we are God's handiwork, created in Christ Jesus to do good works, which God prepared in advance for us to do.

Ephesians 2:10 (NIV)

Being confident of this, that he who began a good work in you will carry it on to completion until the day of Christ Jesus.

Philippians 1:6 (NIV)

GLEN R. LANDIN

*I can do all this through him
who gives me strength.*

Philippians 4:13 (NIV)

The Son is the image of the invisible God, the firstborn over all creation.

Colossians 1:15 (NIV)

GLEN R. LANDIN

And whatever you do, whether in word or deed, do it all in the name of the Lord Jesus, giving thanks to God the Father through him.

Colossians 3:17 (NIV)

For the Lord himself will come down from heaven, with a loud command, with the voice of the archangel and with the trumpet call of God, and the dead in Christ will rise first.

1 Thessalonians 4:16 (NIV)

GLEN R. LANDIN

*Don't let anyone deceive you in any way,
for that day will not come until the rebellion
occurs and the man of lawlessness is revealed,
the man doomed to destruction.*

2 Thessalonians 2:3 (NIV)

For there is one God and one mediator between God and human beings, Christ Jesus, himself human.

1 Timothy 2:5 (NIV)

GLEN R. LANDIN

All Scripture is God-breathed and is useful for teaching, rebuking, correcting and training in righteousness.

2 Timothy 3:16 (NIV)

He saved us, not because of righteous things we had done. but because of his mercy. He saved us through the washing of rebirth and renewal by the Holy Spirit.

Titus 3:5 (NIV)

GLEN R. LANDIN

Confident of your obedience, I write to you, knowing that you will do even more than I ask.

Philemon 1:21 (NIV)

Now faith is being sure of what we hope for and certain of what we do not see.

Hebrews 11:1 (NIV)

GLEN R. LANDIN

And without faith it is impossible to please God, because anyone who comes to him must believe that he exists and that he rewards those who earnestly seek him.

Hebrews 11:6 (NIV)

Therefore confess your sins to each other and pray for each other so that you may be healed. The prayer of a righteous person is powerful and effective.

James 5:16 (NIV)

GLEN R. LANDIN

Now that you have tasted that the Lord is good.

1 Peter 2:3 (NIV)

And you will receive a rich welcome into the eternal kingdom or our Lord and Savior Jesus Christ.

2 Peter 1:11 (NIV)

GLEN R. LANDIN

*If we confess our sins, he is faithful
and just and will forgive us our sins
and purify us from all unrighteousness.*

1 John 1:9 (NIV)

And this is love: that we walk in obedience to his commands. As you have heard from the beginning, his command is that you walk in love.

2 John 1:6 (NIV)

GLEN R. LANDIN

It gave me great joy to have some believers come and testify to your faithfulness to the truth, telling how you continue to walk in it.

3 John 1:3 (NIV)

Keep yourselves in God's love as you wait for the mercy of our Lord Jesus Christ to bring you to eternal life.

Jude 1:21 (NIV)

GLEN R. LANDIN

"I am the Alpha and the Omega," says the Lord God, "who is, and who was, and who is to come, the Almighty."

Revelation 1:8 (NIV)

Here I am! I stand at the door and knock. If anyone hears my voice and opens the door, I will come in and eat with them, and they with me.

Revelation 3:20 (NIV)

GLEN R. LANDIN

Then I saw "a new heaven and a new earth," for the first heaven and the first earth had passed away, and there was no longer any sea.

Revelation 21:1 (NIV)

101 POWERFUL BIBLE VERSES

The grace of the Lord Jesus be with God's people. Amen.

Revelation 22:21 (NIV)

GLEN R. LANDIN

About The Author

Glen Landin continues writing unique and informative books. In this release entitled, "101 powerful bible verses", he combines the most powerful verses from each book of The Bible and includes a bold silhouette cross with each verse.

As a creative writer and author, glen also enjoys interior design, photography, model railroading, visual displays, and traveling to nearby and distant shores.

Through Glen's creative writing skills, using poems, phrases, affirmations, and messages, he inspires, encourages, and motivates people to simply believe in yourself. Because all things are possible to those who believe!

www.ingramcontent.com/pod-product-compliance
Lightning Source LLC
Chambersburg PA
CBHW071720040426
42446CB00011B/2141